D1231507

SHIPPING CONTAINER HOMES

A Beginner's Step-by-Step Guide to Building Your Own Container House With Building Tips and Special Techniques for Plans and Designs

Richie Quincy

TABLE OF CONTENTS

INTRODUCTION

Congratulations on purchasing *Shipping Container Homes,* and thank you for doing so.

In the past few decades, we have seen a variety of unique, innovative, and quirky ideas related to housing. Well, the new generation today is always looking out for something unique when it comes to housing ideas. The days are gone when all the houses in the society looked the same. One of such innovative home ideas that has got all the attention is shipping container homes. You heard it right – homes made from shipping containers. That might sound quite weird as you think of it at first. However, shipping containers can be regarded as one of the best materials for building a home. It is mainly because they are movable, cut table, durable, cheap, and strong.

We will focus mainly on shipping container homes in this guidebook and how you can use the same to make your dream house. From new ideas to designing your home and getting your own container, this book covers all. The process is not that tough, and we are here to help you out. Get your ideas on the line and start designing your own shipping container home with the help of this book.

There are plenty of books on this subject on the market; thanks again for choosing this one! Every effort was made to ensure it is full of as much useful information as possible, please enjoy!

CHAPTER 1

WHAT IS A SHIPPING CONTAINER HOME?

As the name suggests, a shipping container home is a house that is built from steel containers. It is made from big intermodal containers that help in the transportation of goods and merchandise. Shipping containers can be found in two sizes – 20 feet by 8 feet or 40 feet by 8 feet. Talking about the first one, the 20 feet containers measure around 160 square feet long, and the latter containers are 320 square feet long. You have got the option of using such containers as your home, personal office or just combine many of them to create a multi-story residence. Several shipping container home ideas, like small houses, silo housing, or RVs, are getting more popular day by day. It is because of the fact that people today want to opt for alternative designs and ideas to the old styles of conventional home buildings.

What Are The Advantages?

When it comes to shipping container homes, there is a wide range of advantages like they are cost-efficient, customizable, and durable.

Cheaper than traditional accommodation

A shipping container can be bought for as little as $10,000. They are quite cost-effective in nature in comparison to conventional housing. It is because labor and construction materials are less needed. You will get the chance to reduce your living costs in a shipping container by putting into use your DIY skills.

Modular in nature

Container homes can be shipped quite easily and quickly. You can build a house with the use of several containers that range in size from twenty feet to forty feet. You can also include multiple containers for developing a larger house with a dining room, living room, extra floors, and extra bedrooms.

Quick to construct

It is possible to construct your shipping container home in less than one month. You can also employ a contractor for building your home quickly. But if you decide to opt for a contractor, your cost might rise up for creating your dream home. In order to cut off high building costs, you will have to opt for a manufactured container home that can be found from various companies that specializes in off-site buildings.

Durable in nature

Generally, shipping containers are made from Corten steel. Such a kind of self-healing steel helps in supporting cargo at the time of shipping through the water bodies. So, it can be said that homes made from shipping containers will survive better in bad weather compared to standard homes.

Water-resistant and watertight

As shipping containers are manufactured with the aim of shipping and transporting goods of all sizes, and for long distances, they are made indestructible. Shipping containers can easily survive heat, earthquakes, water, and even more.

Highly mobile

You can opt for a specialized shipping provider to collect and relocate a single container house anywhere in the world.

Recycling is always better

Recycled products are one of the best ways of building eco-sustainable homes. You can get expired or "not capable of shipping anymore" containers from anywhere around the world to build your home. At least, reusing another piece of a container is better for the planet.

They are stackable

You have got the option to build a small house or a large house for your whole family. You can keep increasing the size of your house by stacking up containers.

Looks trendy and cool

You have surely come across images of unusual designs of shipping container homes and hotels. That could be the probable reason why you are here. No matter how you organize and design these large containers, you will always have an esthetic design. If you are looking out for a modern and smart home, this is what you need.

Secure in nature

Shipping containers are quite tough to break into, and thus, they can make good secure homes. You can definitely install locks, doors, and windows to make your house more secure. But it won't be that easy for burglars in the first place to get into your house.

Are There Any Disadvantages?

Although there is a wide range of advantages when it comes to shipping container homes, there are certain disadvantages as well that you need to pay attention to.

Not so cheap always

Well, shipping containers themselves cost quite less. However, it is not an inexpensive option all the time to turn them into living houses. If you want to change the layout of your container by adding doors, windows, or partitions, you will need to get the help of an architect to bring your ideas to life. But they will surely cost you a lot.

Getting building permits might not be that easy

Getting the license to build your own shipping container home in certain areas is not that easy. But in the US and outside the US, there are certain locations where shipping container homes can be found and are controlled. You will need to consult with the nearest municipal planning office first for more details related to zoning laws, construction codes, and standards of container homes.

Not that eco-friendly

There are container suppliers who tend to recycle old shipping containers. However, some home buyers have the tendency to turn new containers into their homes. Well, based on the usage experience, used containers tend to be more conscious environmentally. They might have some hazardous chemical history. All such aspects make reusable containers much less suitable for future container homes.

Modern needs can be rigid

If you are not willing to live off the grid, you will have to find an electrician who has the knowledge of building and installing custom electrical systems for homes. Also, you will have to get a plumber to get done with the plumbing work. In case your home location does not have electricity access, you will have to get an installer for adding solar panels on your rooftop.

Need reinforcements

Although storage containers are made from sturdy steel, alterations, like big windows or doors, might jeopardize the structural integrity. Indeed, shipping containers can easily sustain certain environmental conditions. But in case the corner castings are not that strong, the weight of heavy snow can easily make the roof bow if your location snows. You will have to get in touch with a contractor to reinforce the walls and get a sloping roof.

Small in size

Shipping containers are not that large in size. It is true that shipping containers are not that narrow in comparison to small houses on trailers. However, it does not make any kind of huge difference. A shipping container will not be a perfect choice for you if you want complete control over the size of your compact home.

It can get very hot

You will have to look out for ways in which you can keep the sun off from the roof of your container house as there is a chance of solar heat gain. As they are made of steel, lack of insulation might also make it unbearable to stay in your container home at the time of extreme summer heat.

Shipping Container Home And Its Main Features

Shipping container homes are loaded with features. Such homes make a great option for low-cost, fast, and simple installation. Shipping container homes are prefabricated buildings that are designed originally for some other purpose. However, they are suitable for new structures. In relation to this, one container or more than that can be installed easily and quickly. Constructing a conventional home will eat up a lot of your time, money, and effort. Shipping container homes can be regarded as shortcuts where the preliminary task of building a house is cut off. All that you need to do is to design the interior and exterior a bit. And, if you can work on your own, you can save a lot of your money. They are similar to Lego blocks that can be configured and stacked as you like them.

The houses are made of metal walls and will provide you with all the advantages that a metal structure can provide you with.

- Fire resistant

- No wood rot or mold

- Long-lasting and durable

- Protection from harsh weather

They look modern and stylish. If you are willing to build a house that comes with traditional along with futuristic designs, there is hardly anything else that can beat the look of shipping containers. It is mainly aimed at minimalistic designs and architecture. As we have already discussed in the earlier sections, shipping containers are eco-friendly in nature. As you transform a container into your home that is completely safe for the environment, you will be upcycling a container. If needed, you can also recycle your house at a later time as a metal frame. You can look out for various designs and ideas online. Or, you can take the help of an architect for the best house designs and transformations.

CHAPTER 2

TURNING YOUR SHIPPING CONTAINER INTO A HOUSE

At first glance, it might feel that developing and designing a shipping container home is much simpler than building a small traditional house right from scratch. After all, the shell is still present there. It will be better if you can know a bit about developing small traditional houses. You will come to know that almost any type of process, material, and style you opt for, will be disadvantageous and beneficial at the same time. In some aspects, the same also applies while developing a small shipping container home. It can be superior to traditional small houses in some aspects, and it is lower in other ways.

Converting A Shipping Container

Converting a shipping container is not that easy. It will still need your attention and dedication, the same that goes for traditional houses. The whole process goes in various stages. We will discuss the steps in this section that will make the task easier for you.

Stage 1: Designing your home

The very first step while converting a shipping container into your home is to determine the way you want your home to be. Make up your mind which rooms you like, how much space you require, how you can connect the rooms, and so on. Where are you going to place the windows? What about the bathroom, bedroom, and kitchen? Do you need more than one bedroom or bathroom? You will have to think of the logistics as well. The appearance of small porthole windows might fascinate you, but French windows and doors will allow more light in your house. You might want to see your kitchen front facing the bathroom. In that case, you will have to determine whether there is enough space for opening your oven doors or to just step around the breakage without any need to touch the sides. You will have to design your home along with a floor layout so that you can keep the design to normal shipping container floor dimensions – 20 x 8, 40 x 8, and many others.

Stage 2: Consulting an engineer

If you are willing to remove any of the walls, specifically any portion of the two load-bearing walls, you will have to consult an engineer. You will have to get confirmed that the shipping container is sturdy enough. The last that someone would like to build is a building that is not even safe from any angle.

Stage 3: Finishing the design

Once you can properly understand what is and what not might be feasible, finish your home design. You will now have to take certain things into account, like flooring, insulation, framing, energy, and many other things.

Stage 4: Preparing the land

If you have already found a place to develop your shipping container home, the next thing that you will have to do is to level the area out. You will have to create the foundation and make a choice whether or not to lift your container. However, it is always a better option to get in touch with an expert, especially at the time of using several storage containers. But you will have to consider certain alternatives, such as steel plates, concrete plates, concrete strips, or concrete piers. Also, you will have to make sure that there is a direct way of distributing all your containers.

Stage 5: Choosing and buying your shipping container

It is always helpful to order your shipping containers during the early stages. It might also depend on the time that it takes to be delivered. You can select between one-trip, recycled, and brand-new shipping containers. It is suggested to opt for used containers that are of proper quality to be used as a home. You will have to opt for a pre-purchase inspection to check for rusts, bad smoke, and others. Also, finding out what the container was used for can help. The more information you can collect regarding your shipping containers, the better it will be for your home.

Stage 6: Receiving the container

You will need to contract a business crane, freight crane, or forklift for moving your containers to the actual spot. As an alternative, you can ask the container provider to do the task of distribution and placement on your behalf. But you will have to ask beforehand and prepare the building spot. In case you arrange it yourself, you will have to ensure that you handle the overall weight of the shipping containers independent of any kind of equipment that you book. You will also have to make sure of the way in which you will secure the containers to the base, for instance, by hooking or welding it. If you opt for a used shipping container, it will be a good idea to wash it properly first.

Stage 7: Connecting the containers

If you opt for a home design that includes multiple containers, you can hook them up at this stage. Completely depending on how permanent the attachments are, you can use welding, bolts, or clamps.

Stage 8: Structural strengthening

If you need to do any kind of structural strengthening, get in touch with an engineer. But if you need to remove any portion of the shipping containers, it will be a better option to install the reinforcements to avoid any kind of structural problems.

Stage 9: Cutting the openings

Again, if you can properly understand what you are actually doing, you can start cutting out portals, bars, and other walls. At this stage, you can start to make the containers look like a home. You will have to take the help of contractors for doing this job for you. Also, as you will be cutting the containers, you will be losing a part of the anti-corrosive paint. So, you will need to retreat the same. If you tend to block out any of the holes in the openings, you can cover them up for shielding the interior of the house from the elements.

Stage 10: Removing the flooring

In the majority of cases, the floors of the shipping containers face lots of harsh chemicals. You will have to decide the way you feel about this. However, you would certainly want to strip off the floor and get a new one to cover your house from all the harmful toxins. In case you are determined to get a new flowing from the very beginning, you can consider getting high-cube containers as they will provide you with extra headspace.

Stage 11: Frame, sheath, floor, and insulation

Now you will have to attach the insulation, structure, and cover with the internal walls. You would surely want to separate your small home, depending on the place you live in. Coming to insulation, you have got several choices like sheets, spray foam, and many others. It will be a better option to add insulation to the exterior of the container for increasing space usage.

Stage 12: Adding the electrical equipment

As you reach this stage, you will have to get done with all the electrical wiring of your new home. You can get the help of someone who will do the job for you. Determine the number of plug points and the type of electric supply that you are going to use. If your location does not have any kind of electrical supply, you will have to resort to solar energy.

Stage 13: Decorating and moving in

You will be working on all the extras in this stage, like bathrooms, kitchen, water supply, composting toilet, and other elements. After you are done with everything that you had in mind, your small box is good to go. Decorate your new house as you like it and give it your own touch.

How To Plan Your Shipping Container Home?

Here are some suggestions that will help you to get prepared for purchasing your shipping containers and building your container home.

Being willing to pay the price

The majority of people get started with their projects of shipping container homes as they think it will be cheap. Shipping containers will cost only around some thousands of dollars. You will have to take into account the labor costs for customized and complicated production. High-end shipping container houses and large-sized ones might turn out to be as expensive as traditional housing. Before you can start working on your ideas of shipping container homes, you will have to consider the budget. The budget will automatically increase if you want to include all kinds of facilities in your container home and make it lavish.

Contacting the planning department of the city

Although traditional houses are subject to construction and zoning laws, your city council might not have implemented container house legislation. In that case, you will have to request details for non-traditional house rules from the city's planning office. Figure out whether you need to make any kind of special arrangements while building your container home.

Keeping in mind natural lighting while designing

Steel shipping containers will not allow your natural light until you design it so. You can consider adding skylights or glass doors while making the floor plan to make the interior rooms look spacious and bright. In case the storage space is not enough, you can consider getting a high-cube container. They are taller than the traditional shipping containers.

Checking if the containers are in good condition

No matter how you want to design your shipping container home, you need to inspect your shipping containers in person before you opt for buying them. Check out for dents on the sidewalls, rust on the exterior walls, leaks of any kind, and flooring. If you fail to check any of these, the repair cost will be huge at the time of building the house.

Being aware of the limits

As shipping containers are made of heavy steel for carrying goods, they tend to lack the required accommodations that are necessary for a general living environment. Window and door openings, along with snow on the rooftop, will surely hamper the structural integrity of the containers. So, before you make any kind of purchase, make sure to be mindful of the weaknesses of the structure.

What Is The Feeling Of Living In A Shipping Container Home?

Your shipping container home can be as comfortable or as plain as you desire it to be. If you are thinking of building a shipping container home from scratch, you can take the guidance of a builder or architect who is already acquainted with similar projects. They can help you to access the overall system and make you aware of any kind of shortcomings. If you want inspiration or reviews for shipping container homes, you can check out the internet.

CHAPTER 3

SHIPPING CONTAINER HOME FOUNDATION AND ITS TYPES

There are four primary types of foundations that are used for shipping container homes – pier, pile, slab, and strip. Well, there are some other types of foundations; however, these are the most commonly used ones for shipping container houses. We will discuss the outlines of when each of the foundations can be used besides addressing the advantages and disadvantages in this chapter.

Pier Foundation

For several reasons, pier foundations are the most widely used alternative when it comes to shipping container homes. They are quite cheap, easy to build, and are DIY friendly as well. Pier foundations are made of concrete blocks. In order to properly optimize the concrete pressure, each of the concrete piers or blocks uses comes with 50 cm x 50 cm x 50 cm and steel-reinforcing on the inner side. When it comes to shipping container homes, concrete piers are generally used at each corner. You can use two more piers that can be mounted halfway down on either of the container if you use the large 40 feet containers. You will get the chance to save a great deal of money and time on the walls of the piers. Also, you will not need to dig a huge amount of ground for installing the piers.

All you need to do is dig the soil for the piers, typically 50 cm x 50 cm x 50 cm in dimension. In comparison to a baseboard, the entire space under the shipping container needs to be excavated. Pier foundation is by far the most famous base for shipping container homes. It is also the most recommended one out of all.

Pile Foundation

When the foundation of the soil is too thin for supporting the concrete piers, pile foundations are put into use. It is the costliest one out of all. Piles, which are cylindrical rigid steel tubes, are pounded into the soil by the soft soil right before the piles meet a better load-bearing soil. Once the steel piles are properly secured in place, they are capped using a concrete block. They make the ground look the same as it would look if concrete piers are used. Such a type of foundation is not something that DIY-friendly. As special tools are needed for installation, getting a contractor for installing the pile foundation is better.

Slab Foundation

A slab foundation is a common alternative when the ground is soft and permits even distribution of weight. However, building a slab foundation is quite costly and time-intensive when compared to building a pier. If you want to use a base plate, you will need to prepare yourself to dig a lot. Concrete slabs are used over which you can place your shipping containers. The base in this foundation is marginally smaller than the home footprint. For instance, if you install two containers of 40 feet, the base will be 18 feet wide to 42 feet. It will have a somewhat overhanging basis all around the perimeter of the shipping container. One of the primary advantages of this kind of foundation is that there will be no empty gap in your home base. So, it can be said that a slab foundation can provide your house with a stable backbone. It also helps in avoiding any kind of complication related to termites.

But slab foundations are not that cheap as they use extra mortar along with the huge amount of space that needs to be excavated. It can also be used in cooler conditions where freezing is not an issue. But as the temperature of the surface falls below the interior temperature, the risk of heat loss also increases. It is because the shipping containers can easily conduct heat to the soil, which can move heat in comparison to convection into the air. Keep in mind that access to the service lines will be limited when concrete is attached to the slab foundation. Whenever there is a leakage of water lines, you will have to replace the concrete for providing access to the leaking lines. If you use a pier foundation, you can also access the power lines.

Strip Foundation

Also known as a trench base, it is a mixture of slab and pier foundation. The strip foundation is a surface of the concrete that is laid for holding the containers. The band of the strips is generally 4 feet tall and 1 – 2 feet wide. The strip can either run all around the circumference of the container or can also be placed at the top and bottom of the shipping containers. It is a suitable option when you want something less expensive for the foundation but has a smaller base. A rubble-strip foundation of loose stones right under the concrete strips can be used in all those areas where the ground soil is quite damp because of a huge amount of moisture. Also, these stones help water to flow and drain properly. But in comparison to any of the other foundation options, strip foundation is the most fragile one of the lot. As they come with a shallow shape, the strip bases are only suitable for small to medium constructions.

It is the most important factor for a shipping container home to have a stable, clean, and solid base. In strip foundation, there are three types of used foundations that come with different cost rates. The first foundation is a trench floor. It is constructed of brick and block masonry. It is filled with concrete. A base of somewhat $5,000 can easily accommodate larger containers. The second one is a pier foundation. A pier foundation of $5,000 is enough for holding a big shipping container on a site where the soil is firm. The last one is the slab foundation which is the costliest of all. It will cost you around $6,000 as it uses both steel and concrete bars for stabilizing the home.

Attaching Shipping Containers To The Foundation

The most widely used method of connecting the shipping containers to the pad of foundation is by using a steel plate. The cast alternative includes pushing down a steel plate with anchors onto the wet concrete. Once the anchors are mounted, you will have to epoxy them in place. You can also use mechanical anchors; however, they are not that necessary all the time. Also, they are less powerful in nature and are not that much recommended. In any of the cases, you are looking out for a flat level of a concrete plate for complementing the four fittings of the corners on each container. If the concrete has properly dried or healed, you can set the shipping containers on steel plates. Now, you can solder them both together. There are people who tend to place the shipping containers directly on the floors. In such instances, tremendous weight is deposited. It is more or less alright; however, you are also needed to be aware of tornados and flooding that can easily drive a loose container.

Concrete Quality To Be Used For Foundation

You will come to know whether you need a slab base or a concrete pier in this section. When someone decides to go for a concrete box, the next big question that arises is the strength of the concrete that needs to be used. Geotechnical engineers determine the concrete strength that you need to use for your home. The strength of concrete is known as the C rating. The most widely used all-purpose concrete, concrete C15, consists of one part of cement, five parts of gravel, and two parts of sand. The more cement is used, the stronger the concrete will be. For instance, C30 is a super-strong concrete that includes one part of cement, three parts of gravel, and two parts of sand. If you need to mix tiny amounts, it can be done using your hands. You can also opt for a cement mixer.

Keep in mind that if you mix the concrete by yourself, ensure that the components are properly mixed. In case you fail to do that, the concrete strength will get reduced significantly. You just need to count the cubic meters of your foundation for determining the concrete that you will need. For instance, if you need to find out the required amount of concrete for 10 feet deep and 22 feet long base plate, multiply 22 x 10 x 2. The quantity of concrete that you will need is 440 cubic feet.

If you put concrete in very hot weather, make sure that you prepare the site before pouring the concrete. You can place temporary shades to block all the direct sunlight. Also, you will have to spray the ground with cold water right before pouring the concrete. Another great tip is to pour concrete either early in the morning or late in the evening to prevent excessive temperatures.

CHAPTER 4

COSTING OF BUILDING A SHIPPING CONTAINER HOME

The very thought of living in a house that is made of shipping containers might sound quite enticing and intimidating. Shipping container homes can be considered as the new housing alternative that seems quite new and youthful. There are people who think that building a house using shipping containers is as easy and simple as stacking bricks. It would seem like this to anyone who sees it from the outside only. Also, such beliefs contribute to the idea that shipping container homes are much less expensive in comparison to developing a traditional home. But is it for real? The answer is "no." Developing shipping container homes are not that cheap necessarily than building any kind of traditional house; however, it can be. Scale, architecture, place, and interior options are some of the major factors that tend to affect the expenses of a project.

The container you opt for will cost around $1,500 for small-sized containers to $6,000 for the larger and newer ones. New containers will obviously cost you more in comparison to the old shipping containers. A typical shipping container includes metal outer walls, a flat roof, and a metal frame that acts as the overall foundation of your home. Often, all these features are referred to as cost savings. But no one tries to see that you will also have to pay for shipping the containers to the location, interior finishes, and also insulation. You will also have to pay a great sum for the place or ground.

On the contrary, shipping container homes are generally built on all those lands that are not that suitable for any kind of normal condition. In case the soil is steep and rocky, you can only build a traditional house after you get done with intensive site work. Shipping container homes can be easily built in such locations with sturdy pilings in place of going for the costly drilling.

Shipping Container Costings

The value of an entire shipping container home can be easily broken down by determining the price of each of the containers separately. Generally, shipping container costs are dictated by their quality and size. The larger is the scale of a container, the more will be the amount. Also, the newer is the container, the costlier it will be. Any kind of used container generally costs around $1,500 in the US. The larger 40 feet ones, which are the most suitable ones for larger homes, can cost you around $2,500 to $4,000 for the used ones. A new 40 feet container will cost you around $6,000. With that said, the majority of people in the US opt for buying each of the containers for $1,500 to $4,000. They go for five to six containers with which a proper house can be built easily.

Building A Home

Now that you know how much each of the containers for your house will cost, you can progress to the other points of construction. At this stage, you will have to take into account the cost of the land, the domestic installations for the home, and the scheme of insulation.

Land price for shipping container homes

The size of your house, along with the location, will define the land cost for your shipping container home. In case you have your site of construction ready already, there is nothing to be concerned about spending a lot of money. But if you do not have the site ready for your home, you can now add it to your budget estimates. Keep in mind that the cost of the land will be much higher in comparison to the costing of your shipping containers.

Paying Attention To Other Home Improvements

As you estimate the cost of your shipping container home, you will have to take into account the cost of other home improvement services as well. Installation of doors, screens, and hardware will cost you around $6,000. It can be more or less depending on how you want to design and set up your home. Any kind of electrical work and plumbing will cost you about $7,000. Roofing and flooring can be used in various configurations. However, the cost will vary around $3,000 and $5,000. The last thing that you will have to keep in mind is the cost of painting and finishes. It will cost you around $5,000. Now, you might have the question in mind: what is the overall cost of building a shipping container home? Well, it is a complex subject where there are several factors for you to consider. You can keep in mind a few numbers for easing up your task of costing.

- A shipping container at the very bottom will cost you around $1,400 to $6,000 at the top.

- A very small container home will cost around $10,000 to $40,000 from anywhere.

- A large shipping container home can cost you easily around $100,000.

What are things that might lead to major price disparities for the same-sized home?

There are certain factors that might impact the pricing of a shipping container home. Do you want to go for an eco-friendlier option? In several cases, a huge amount of repair and even washing might be needed. Also, the scale and consistency of the container itself play a huge role. How many containers are you opting for, and how many can be shipped at once? Also, the manufacturing and welding necessary for completing the house, depending on the specifications, will result in additional costs. You might need to integrate power and plumbing along with wastewater. You also have the choice of mounting the electrical wires. In that case, it will add up to extra costs. You might need to expand on the vacant space for clearing the property for utilities. It might turn out to be costly than the actual house construction of all such utilities. You will have to determine the cost of the external and internal finishing of the containers. The size and number of windows and doors that you want to install will increase the cost. The kind of insulation that you opt for will also affect the overall costing of your shipping container home.

The pricing of a shipping container house also impacts the amount of work you plan to do with a contractor. You have got the option of saving a lot of money by doing a number of jobs alone. However, it will cost you a great deal of your expertise and time. But the final verdict is that shipping container homes can be made affordable than traditional homes. How many alternatives are there to build your own house with a cost of $10,000? Well, I am sure you will not find any.

Are Shipping Container Homes Easier To Build?

Shipping container homes are generally constructed much faster than any kind of traditional home. The smallest and most basic homes can be built in a few days or weeks. It all depends on the amount of finishing work that is needed by the style. If you opt for complex designs and features, it can take somewhat around a few months to finish. If you want the fastest sort of shipping container homes, you can look out for companies that fabricate most of the construction offsite right before delivering the same to your location. Such kinds of prefab-style container homes are generally small in size. However, they come assembled with everything that you will require to move in right away.

How Eco-Friendly Container Homes Can Be?

Although we have said that shipping container houses are eco-friendly, there are certain contentions here. While shipping containers are recyclable and reusable, lightly used containers are generally upcycled for container homes. Also, shipping containers are constructed to be quite solid to the point that they are enough to be used for residential housing. If shipping containers are used to their full potential, the world would have been much cleaner. However, in real life, the transportation of containers back from their destination ports to the origin ports might turn out to be unmanageable in terms of cost. There are businesses that do not want to pay such costs. For dealing with all such prices, there are companies who tend to abandon shipping containers completely. They also engage in replacing them.

So, if the containers just sit there, they can easily overwhelm the overall scenery and just ruin it. It is always a better option from the aspect of the environment to use them as container homes instead of abandoning them.

How Large Shipping Container Homes Can Be?

The most common dimensions are 20 feet by 8 feet and 40 feet by 8 feet. But relying on your selection, you will have either 160 square feet or 320 square feet of living space. The height of the containers is around 8.5 feet, but you can increase the same by customizing your containers. Also, you have the choice of joining multiple containers for increasing the living area.

CHAPTER 5

SHIPPING CONTAINER HOME AND SAFETY

There are people who have already fallen in deep love with the idea of building a shipping container home because of the affordability along with other benefits. Shipping container homes are quite cheaper, as we already know, and are also durable, efficient, and eco-friendly in comparison to traditional homes. There are also people who claim that shipping containers are great for pop-up stores, suites, and industrial spaces. However, no matter what kinds of incredible features they offer, is it actually safe to live in shipping container homes? There are even families who are building shipping container homes. Is it safe for children?

Are Shipping Container Homes Safe?

It will take a lot of adjustments to live inside a shipping container home. You will have to weigh a number of considerations, whether it fits with all your needs. Efficiency, durability, and affordability cannot be regarded as anything if you do not feel comfortable inside your container home. One of the primary advantages of shipping container homes is their longevity. But are there any other aspects that you need to consider while planning to live in a shipping container for a long time? Sometimes, you just cannot be sure what is in a used shipping container – from dangerous raw chemicals to innocuous household products. The finishes and paints that are used on shipping containers are meant for the transportation of commercial goods across the coast. They are not made for private households.

Harmful chemicals in containers

One of the most common safety issues that can be related to shipping containers is the harmful toxic chemicals that are applied to them. The wooden floors are generally treated with hazardous and heavy pesticides so that the shipped goods are safe at the time of transportation. Also, there are shipping containers that are o coated with paint, not at all great for human living. So, you will have to address the problem of used shipping containers. As you opt for second-hand containers, the harmful chemicals will be there. What can be done regarding this? Firstly, you will have to inquire from the actual manufacturer whether the shipping container is treated using harmful chemicals. If you do not know how to track the manufacturer, you will get an identification number on the body of the container that can help you.

You have got the option of removing the actual flooring and replacing the same with a brand new one. Also, you can remove the coating of paint and use another new coating. After all this, the adequate and best solution is to use foam insulation to protect your family and yourself from harmful chemicals. If you are very much worried about toxic chemicals, you can get new shipping containers.

But that will increase your overall costing and will also decrease the purpose of eco-friendliness.

Disaster-Proof

The next big thing that the majority of people are curious about is whether shipping container homes are disaster-proof or not. We all have seen on the news how natural disasters ruin conventional homes so easily. However, shipping containers stay completely intact. It is because shipping containers are made in a way so that they can withstand a load of about 25 – 30 tons. So, it is no surprise how they can withstand all kinds of natural disasters. There are also various claims that prove home containers to be flood-proof and hurricane-resistant because of the foundations and anchors of the containers.

Secured Container Homes

Some of the shipping container homeowners want to use the containers as a cabin and just place the same in the wilderness. So, it is important for them to know how secured shipping container homes are. It is of primary concern when they just tend to leave the container homes as it is for months. Is it possible for someone to break in? Well, you need to give it a thought regarding the actual functioning of the shipping containers. They are designed in a way that makes them airtight and impenetrable for transporting all types of goods. So, it can be said that shipping containers are quite safe in nature. However, if you tend to remove the primary parts or portions of the containers for modification, the level of security lessens.

The overall security of shipping container homes is more or less like conventional homes. So, if you want to use it as a cabin, you will need to maintain the actual structure of the containers. It is okay to have doors and windows behind the actual containers. In this way, you will get the chance to securely lock and seal the door of the container.

Getting A Perfect System Of Insulation

Shipping container homes can turn out to be excessively cold in the winter season and extremely hot during the summer season. In order to make them livable and completely safe for the homeowners, it is necessary to get a proper insulation system in place. When it comes to insulation, there are several options that you can choose from. One of the primary concerns while getting an insulation system is the wall depth. The insulation might take up a great amount of space. There are people who recommend spray foam insulation as it is one of the easiest methods of insulating your container home. However, if you think that the other options of insulation will be better for your needs, go for them. Many people tend to worry that their container homes will be a dead heat trap that will surely make their housing experience unpleasant. Well, prefabricated containers can be quite spacious and more energy-efficient in comparison to conventional homes.

One of the primary reasons why modified shipping containers are used for building homes or workplaces is because of their robustness. They can easily protect you from adverse weather conditions.

Strong And Sturdy

Shipping containers are made of steel which makes them quite durable and tough. They are designed in a way so that they can deal with severe weather conditions both on land and at sea, ensuring the survival of the cargo. Such containers are exposed at sea too strong winds and high waves. If shipping containers can survive such dangerous conditions, they can also endure the majority of the storms as you convert them into your home. You will have to remove some of the portions for creating openings for windows and doors. But manufacturers employ various creative methods to maintain a balance between adding windows and doors and thus maintaining proper structural integrity. Shipping containers that are modified can easily withstand high winds and storms even without any kind of bolting.

Although when left unsecured, standalone containers can withstand winds of up to 100 mph. If you fasten to a proper foundation, it will increase the security and safety of your container home that can withstand wind of up to 170 mph. All of this makes shipping container modifications a superb option for all those who live in extreme weather conditions.

Secure as conventional homes

Shipping containers are designed to provide an impenetrable and airtight option for transportation of global freight. Well, you can regard them as one of the safest storage systems. If you change the container shape for doors and windows, removing metal from the container body will decrease the degree of its safety. But with the installation of good windows and doors, you can make your shipping container home as secure as any other conventional home. Safety can also be improved with the usage of alarm systems. If you want to get the maximum security, maybe because it is placed at some remote location, it will be better for you to preserve the container's actual configuration. Try to place the windows and doors on the backside so that you can lock the actual doors.

Impenetrable to pests

Shipping containers are resistant to insects and rodents because of the steel structure. Even when you install wooden floors or outer walls, the interior construction will still be of steel, and no insect can penetrate. Indeed, termites might tend to damage the external or internal sides of the house; the steel cannot be penetrated. Thus, it ensures the structural integrity of the home.

CHAPTER 6

INSULATING YOUR SHIPPING CONTAINER HOME

We already know that shipping containers are made of steel, and they can easily conduct heat and cold. It indicates that if your location is very hot, you might get baked in the extreme heat. Also, if your location is cold, you might end up freezing. Additionally, you need to consider the condensation effects on your home. If you fail to provide adequate protection, you might end up with mold or rust in your home. So, it is clear that you need some proper insulation. You might feel that there is no need to get insulation for your home, and it is only an extra expenditure. However, one thing is guaranteed, the first snowfall in winter or the first heat of the summer will surely change your mind. In the long run, it will be more cost-effective to insulate your container home than just leaving it as it is. All the methods of insulation that you might consider will rely on one factor the climate and temperature of the area.

In case the location in which you live is quite cold, you will require lots of insulation not only for keeping your house warm but also for preventing condensation. Condensation might result in mold and rust. Besides cold, if you experience a lot of rainfall, you will require foam insulation in order to prevent the vapor from getting in. On the contrary, if your area is dry and hot, you will not require that much insulation as you would need in a cold climate. Let us have a look at some of the insulation options, how to use them, and the one that will suit you the best.

Foam Insulation

Spray foam insulation comes with a wide range of benefits if you are opting for it. To start with, it is the fastest method of insulating your container home. The barrier that is provided by this kind of insulation is seamless. It can easily prevent mold and rust. Also, it can provide your home with the highest R rating, which indicates the extent to which the insulation can resist the flow of heat. You can spray this form of insulation even in gaps. The only downside of this form of insulation is that it might be a bit expensive.

Additionally, it might end up being messy than other methods of insulation. As you apply spray foam, make sure that you spray not only the interior and exterior walls but also the space underneath the shipping containers. It will make sure that moisture does not get in the way. One of the most effective spray foam insulation is closed-cell polyurethane foam. If you want to make the exterior walls more attractive, you can paint the insulation once it gets set.

Insulation Panels

If you want to opt for panel insulation, you will need to have stud walls for fitting. For all those who are fond of a DIY approach, this can be regarded as the best option for insulation. You can get the panels in various predefined sizes and can also be fit in the gaps in stud walling. Also, this form of insulation is quicker to fit in comparison to other types of insulation. But this form of insulation might turn out to be a bit expensive. One thing that you will have to keep in mind is that panel insulation comes with smaller depth; however, it has a great insulating value. So, if foam insulation seems too expensive for you, you can opt for panel insulation which you can get at a comparatively lower price. It will also ensure that the insulation thickness is at a minimum.

Blanket Insulation

Blanket insulation can be regarded as one of the cheapest options out of the lot. Just like panel insulation, this form of insulation also requires stud walls for fitting. It is also quite a fast method as once the stud walls are up, the insulation can be installed in the gaps fast. One of the most common types of blanket insulation is rock wool. An important that you will have to keep in mind is that this form of insulation is often made of fiberglass, and so you will have to handle the same with care. As this is the cheapest option of insulation, in case you are working on a very tight budget, this can be the best bet.

Eco-Friendly Insulation Options

As the main reason people opt for shipping container homes is that they are eco-friendly, there are eco-friendly insulation options.

Wool

Wool insulation is more or less like blanket insulation. However, the material makes the main difference which is sheep wool in place of fiberglass. Wool insulation does not come with much effectivity in comparison to blanket insulation.

Cotton

It is similar to wool insulation as it can be considered as a type of blanket insulation. It uses recycled clothes that are made of cotton. Well, it is a renewable option and can be developed quite fast. You will have to keep in mind that cotton insulation can be more expensive than fiberglass.

Mud walls

Mud is not only a superb option for insulation but can also be used for building a complete house. Well, keeping that aside, mud can be used for keeping all the heat outside your home in hot and dry climates. Mud can be used on the roof along with the walls of the shipping containers. As you apply mud on the external walls, make sure that you use battens to help the mud layer stay stuck. But if your home location receives heavy rainfall, mud insulation is not a great idea. It can just flow off during heavy rains.

Factors To Keep In Mind At The Time Of Insulation

Insulation of your shipping container home is an important step in the overall process of construction if you want to make your home livable and safe. If you fail to install proper insulation, the chances are high that you will either freeze in cold climates or get baked in hot climates. It is because the heat and cold can get easily transported through the steel. While insulating your container home, there are certain things that you will have to keep in mind.

The climate of your container home

All kinds of decisions related to insulation start from the environment. Insulation helps in retaining internal temperature and external weather. The more extreme you tend to face, the more insulation you seek. In case you build your home in a temperate climate, weatherproofing your home over insulation can be focused on. Dry and wet temperatures lead to differences in insulation issues. However, the wet conditions might turn out to be the most hazardous for a house made of steel. Water will tend to rust the steel and will slowly ruin the house. You will have to focus on removing water from the steel. You will surely not want steel condensation to hamper the interior of your home.

Contractor or DIY for insulating your shipping container home

Shipping container homes are quite common among all those who love DIY approaches. It is also because of the fact that the need for qualified work can be cut off with shipping container homes. You will have to decide the amount of work that you would like to do yourself before planning your house. A DIY home will always cost less. But your construction opportunities might get limited because of your skills.

Vapor barrier

Box architecture tends to perform better than conventional buildings because of the fact how steel boxes perform in extreme wet conditions. The interior walls of shipping containers tend to condense water or sweat. Water can induce rusting of the steel, and your house can worsen even quickly. If you have any kind of internal building material, like drywall or timber, it might get destroyed. You can create a steam barrier in several ways. You can use wraps inside your home. The easiest way of installing wraps is a DIY project. But it does not fix the problem of water condensation to a great extent. Spray foam can provide a great seal on the steel; however, the additives are not that safe to use. So, it is not a perfect fit for the amateurs.

Cooling, heating, or both

Both cooling and heating come with several options for insulation. A shipping container home can act as a greenhouse in the heat of summer days. The sunlight requires substantial shielding where there is no form of radiant obstruction. It needs a material that will absorb all the heat and make sure that the heat does not affect the internal temperature. There are homeowners who tend to use specialized colors or reflective materials on the external areas of the containers. A living roof or a rooftop greenhouse can help in retaining radiant warmth during the summer days. When the climate is cold, you will want two primary things – drawing the sun's radiant heat and deterring the heat from escaping your home. You will have to find a spot with enough sunlight followed by a lining of the external areas of your home with materials that are non-reflective.

Heat loss takes place in two primary areas: the walls and the roof. Having a glass panel can lose about ten times more heat than an insulated wall. The more windows you plan to install, the more walls you will need to insulate. When you have well-planned windows and a properly isolated roof, you can keep a great amount of heat inside your home.

Vacation home or permanent residence

There are people who tend to build container homes as three-season holiday spots. They tend to use the container homes in spring, summer, and autumn when the outside weather is quite hot. However, they close their homes during winters. If you are not going to use your container home at high temperatures, like cold weather, you can build your house with less insulation and less heating capacity.

Home layout

The surface area can influence the amount of heat that your shipping container will reach or exit. The greater is the surface area, the more insulation you will need. One big rectangle or square is an effective form as it minimizes the overall ratio of floor and inner space. There are people who tend to make their shipping container homes in irregular shapes. Keep in mind that the more irregular your house, the more amount of insulation you will need.

Eco-friendly alternatives

There are people who want to build shipping container homes because of the eco-friendly nature of container homes. Shipping containers get recycled themselves. However, there are several insulation products that are completely safe for the environment. We have already discussed the eco-friendly alternatives in the earlier sections. But recycled insulation cannot be that sustainable as the original products. If you want to make your home completely eco-friendly, you will have to study the process of manufacturing the insulation options to make sure they are efficient and clean.

External or internal solution

Shipping containers can easily restrict the space that you have. The standard containers are 8.5 feet high and 8 feet wide. The amount of internal space that you have will reduce all your insulation choices. You will have to keep a distance between the steel and the inner walls as you start adding insulation inside your house. It will also reduce the size of the rooms by several inches on the floor, walls, and ceiling. But internal insulation is less costly and is also easier to install in comparison to external insulation. If you opt for external insulation, you can maximize the size of your home. However, external insulation will need more repairs. Effective insulation decisions will help in reducing the cooling or heating costs. It will also help in making your home more eco-friendly.

Cooling Your Container Home

Besides insulation, cooling and heating have several options. If you want to protect your home from the summer heat, you can create a living roof. It is nothing but a simple greenhouse on the container home roof that consists of plants and grasses. Plants and soils cannot be regarded as the perfect insulators; however, if your location is warm, they can provide you the needed help to block out solar radiation. It can be said that a living roof is not an insulation substitute but a complement to it. Green or living roofs also come with the extra advantage of being appealing visually. If seen from the air, your container home would seem like another piece of land. Although it is not the best solution when it comes to insulation, it is an eco-friendly alternative that tends to add an extra layer of security.

Home Insulation During Cold Spell

If your container home is located in a cold place, you need to get it ready for the winter months.

- **Keeping the HVAC system and furnace in good order:** Try to change the filters of your HVAC system on a monthly basis, especially if you use it extensively during the winter months. It will not only enhance the quality of the air, but it will also help the machine to run smoothly. In order to optimize the airflow in the rooms, keep obstructions, like furniture and tables, away from the air vents.

- **Examining the heating areas:** In which rooms you spend most of your time? In case you have a second or even a third heating and cooling zone in the house, remember that they are not required to be set in the exact same way. You can reduce the temperature of the rooms that you do not visit that much. Close the doors to trap the heat where you require it the most instead of allowing it to circulate in empty spaces.

- **Making your house more comfortable:** Indoor lighting is extremely necessary while moving from fall to spring. You can follow certain tips for making your home brighter and hotter as you approach the winter season.
  1. You can replace sheers with thicker curtains. If you have drafty walls, you will surely not regret compromising

light by investing in cellular shades to hold the heat in and keep the cold out.

2. Keep the windows and doors closed. In order to make a seal and prevent air exchange, try to wrap foam weather stripping around the inside area of your doors.

3. You can also apply insulation coating to the doors and windows.

Can A Roof Be Added To Your Shipping Container Home?

When you tend to strengthen the corners of shipping containers, the structural stability of the original roof might get reduced. Adding extra roofing to your container home can help in altering the temperature to a great extent. Also, adding a roof helps in increasing the esthetic look of your home. There are various types of roofs when it comes to shipping container homes, like sloping roofs, flat roofs, living roofs, and roof terraces. A flat roof is the best option if you are looking out for the quickest, easiest, and cheapest roof option. However, they might turn out to be difficult to maintain. You can opt for a pitched roof if you live in a location of heavy snow and precipitation. Hips, skillions, and gambrels are the most common examples.

Another great roof option is the dach terrace. It is an imaginative flat area that is constructed on top of the original roof. It can help in extending the already occupied spaces. If you want to extend your living room, outside parking, or lounger areas, you can opt for additional roofing.

It is always suggested to plan your home insulation in advance before you start working on your container house. One small mistake can cost you heavily, besides hampering the condition of your shipping container home.

CHAPTER 7

THINGS TO KEEP IN MIND

It is quite easy to see why the idea of shipping container homes is getting popular day by day. The entire thing seems to be very easy and simple. All that you need to do is to get a container or a number of containers. You can stack the containers or just join them side by side for more rooms. Sounds quite simple, right? Well, it is not that simple. There are a number of factors that you need to consider while using shipping containers for your home. The first thing that you will have to understand is that they were never meant to build homes. Their sole purpose is to transport cargo. There are a few tips that can help you in designing and building a proper shipping container home with the least amount of hassle.

Seeing Before Buying

It can be regarded as one of the best tips. The company that you choose to get your containers from will always reassure you that the containers are in perfect condition. However, keep in mind that shipping containers are used for the transportation of goods in all probable conditions – from rough seas to bad roads. Although they are built durable enough for dealing with all such conditions, they might turn out to be really worn out with extensive usage. It is always suggested to check the containers before you opt for buying them. If you do not want to experience any kind of bad or distressing things afterward at the time of construction, you can consider this advice to be the golden one.

Spending A Bit Extra

In case you opt for buying some extensively used shipping containers, the chances are high that you might lament later. So, it is suggested all the time to opt for a bit extra. You can get one-trip containers, and they are easily available as well. Also, they do not cost much in comparison to used containers. The most important thing is that they are brand new. So, you will not need to worry about the state of the containers that you opt for. With that said, the first piece of advice will always be at the top and be the golden one. Always try to see what you are purchasing before you actually buy them.

Getting Idea About The Local Regulations

It will always depend on the size of the containers that you use. However, that will again depend on the minimum size that is needed for getting a building permit. In simple terms, every country in the world has its own regulations and rules. You will not only need to think about the council rules, but there are various laws that indicate what is the perfect building material and what is not, who all can build container homes, and so on. Also, you will have to take into account the various weather and climate patterns. What fits great for Denmark, for instance, will surely not fit great for Chile, and vice versa. You will have to make up your mind about the location of your shipping container home and then study the local regulations. You need to be aware of all those things that you can do and cannot do, the permits you need to get, and others.

Finding Someone To Take Care Of Everything

It is quite essential to get a person or a company who can take you through the overall process, right from start to finish. It indicates that the person who designs and modifies the exterior will also handle all the interior tasks. It is something that will make complete sense when you try to think about it. A company that deals with building shipping container homes will have all the ideas regarding the structure of various types of homes. They can also incorporate their designs into the interior that will match with the exterior and work great on a structural basis. It also indicates that being the homeowner, you will not have to remember all those stuff that you have no idea about. Indeed, there a big problem with this advice. There are only a few numbers of companies or people who can handle this task for you. It will also depend on your location, your budget, and several other similar considerations.

Knowing About Shipping Container Structures

It is something that you just cannot allow yourself to forget. As already said earlier, shipping containers are meant for the transportation of goods. It is not at all meant for the construction of homes. The roof of the majority of shipping containers is made thin and can get dents very easily. The container walls act as both load bearers and braces. All of this will be extremely important when you think about cutting out wall portions to install windows and doors. The more portions are removed, the lesser load the wall can bear. If you tend to remove a great portion of the walls, the whole thing will just collapse. It is nothing but simple physics. You will have to keep in mind that for every piece you decide to cut off from the walls, you will have to compensate the same somewhere else.

Minimizing Welding Work

As we are talking about a metal box, you will have to opt for welding some of the parts at some point. But keep in mind that welding might turn out to be a costly thing. Also, it will need a certain level of expertise that you will probably not possess. Another negative thing is that the process of welding will take up a lot of time. So, it will be better for you if you can keep the task of welding to a minimum while setting up your container home. Indeed, you will have to opt for welding where it is needed. But you will have to figure out ways how you can manage the same.

Thinking About The Insulation

Shipping containers are made of steel. It is a great conductor of cold and heat. In case you live in a place of extreme cold, you might end up freezing in your home. Another huge problem when it comes to lower temperatures is condensation. As the interior of your home will be warmer than the outside, the cold air will tend to condense and result in water droplets on the walls. After some time, it will result in rust. When it is about higher temperatures, you might get baked inside your home. You will have to properly study the insulation of your container home so that the walls do not end up getting rust.

Planning About Plumbing

No matter which kind of home you build for yourself, plumbing is extremely important. When you get an already constructed traditional house, you will get everything regarding plumbing already done. However, the same cannot be said for shipping container homes. It is nothing but a rectangular metal box. You will have to discuss with your designer and make sure where you want to get the plumbing. Also, you will have to be aware of the kind of plumbing that the container can handle. In case you want to stack shipping containers for a bigger building and more rooms, you can consider cutting out plumbing compartments so that that the plumbing pipes can run easily. Consult with your designer for the best results.

CHAPTER 8

SITE PREPARATION

There is a great amount of site work that needs to be done before you can start working on your shipping container home. If you fail to think about and execute all these in the early stages of the project, you might have to deal with some costly rework at a later stage. At the topmost level, the preparation and site planning you opt for at this stage is mainly intended to make sure that the land is completely prepared for the building site. You will need to opt for site preparation so that the land is ready for the containers. There are several factors that you need to consider while preparing the site for your container home.

Deciding The Location

Before you can make your mind to start working on the actual home, you will have to determine where you want to place your shipping containers.

Shade and sun

Depending on the climate, the sun might turn out to be both a curse and a blessing. It might end up warming you up on a cool morning. However, it might also blind you while having your morning beverage. It can deliver natural and soft lighting in the interior spaces; however, it might also result in a solar thermal gain that will cost you extra air conditioning. As you begin narrowing down the probable building sites on the property, try to figure out the way in which the sun interacts with every area at various times of the day. Shades from nearby bushes and trees can make some huge differences. Keep in mind that the shade will get reduced when deciduous trees start shedding their leaves during winter and fall.

Site Work

Under the section of site work, you will be considering all sorts of physical work that you will need to get done with the building site along with the surrounding areas. Relying on the dirt type that needs to be removed, the utilities need to be installed, and the direction of approach, it will make more sense to do one thing at a time.

Staking and marking

The first step is to mark all the corners where you will be placing your shipping containers. You will also have to mark the locations of the existing and planned utilities, other buildings, roads, etc. For a part of this, you might have to get in touch with some utility locating companies that can assist you to know where you have the gas pipelines, water mains, or some other buried utilities. Such utilities are not affiliated with the project; however, they just pass through your property. You can use ground marking paints for a better idea, along with wooden stakes. You can join them with strings to get a better picture of the larger areas. After you are done with marking the building site, you will know where you have to work for the next steps.

Grubbing and clearing

In this step, you will have to clear all sorts of debris, vegetation, and obstacles from the marked areas. It will involve the removal of bushes, trees, rocks, junk, and other things that might get in your way. It can be done easily by getting a contractor. However, if you want to save money, you can do it yourself. The more is the vegetation in your area, the more you will have to work. You will also have to think about what to do with all the things that you collect. You can cut the vegetation into small pieces and use them for compost. The big pieces can be used as firewood. You can also pile up everything and bury them, burn them, or haul them away.

Grading, cutting, filling

After you are done with clearing out everything that comes in your way of the building site, you can start seeing what you need to work with. Relying on the type of foundation that you have opted for, a building site that is uneven in nature might turn out to be a problem for you. But if you are opting for slab foundation or something of that sort, you will have to do some grading work and develop a properly leveled building pad. In this stage, you will also have to think about your drainage planning. To control the water flow, you might have to add berms and swales to protect the shipping containers and redirect water from the same. Also, you will have to start working on the access road. You will need to pick a route that is right for you.

You might have to install bridges, culverts, or low-water crossings if there is any place where water flows.

Soil Types

The soil of your building site might be filled with clay or sandy. Also, it might be filled up with rocks or even solid rocks. What you need to know is that each of the soil types can handle weight in different ways. So, it is extremely important to know what the soil type of your location can actually handle before starting on the plans.

Gravel

It is a coarse-grained material that can provide you with superb drainage. It is quite easy to dig out to your required depth and also level it for the foundation of your home.

Rock

Working with a rocky surface might turn out to be a bit challenging. However, it will be a blessing for you if the building site is a slab of rock. All you need to do is to strip any soil surface, level the pad, and you are ready to go. Rock comes with some great load-bearing capacity. It can also support any kind of foundation. If your contractor still recommends you to use supports, you can opt for concrete piers. All you need to do is to drill through the rock and then go down to the recommended depth. After that, just frame and pour.

Sandy soil

It is composed of fine-grained particles, often with some rock and gravel mixed in. It can support a huge amount of weight only if the weight is distributed over a large area.

Clay

It is very fine-grained and can hold a lot of water. Your contractor might ask you to dig down the clay part and then backfill with other suitable soil. You can opt for a concrete pile foundation for clay soil.

Septic And Sewer

If your home location offers access to some nearby sewer lines, you will have to determine the cost along with the process of tying in. For rural areas, a septic system might be your only available option. The upfront cost of installing a septic system is quite high than a sewer connection. However, getting a septic system will cut off the cost of the monthly fee that is associated with the sewer connection.

The majority of septic systems include a buried tank or several tanks along with a buried line with sprinklers or leach pipes. Consult with your contractor to find a good location for your septic system.

You will have to pay proper attention to the site preparation as it will form the base of your entire shipping container home. Even the smallest mistakes might cost you a huge sum afterward.

CHAPTER 9

RECEIVING YOUR CONTAINER

You are done with purchasing your shipping containers, and now you are all set to receive them. However, just like every other thing, there are certain considerations that you need to pay attention to before the delivery truck shows up. Before you schedule the delivery of your shipping containers, ensure that the home location is already prepared. You will also have to pay attention to zoning regulations and check permits. Here are a few of the steps that you will have to follow to make sure that the delivery of your containers runs smoothly.

Communicate

Proper communication with the delivery driver in the first place is something that you can never overlook. Before the driver shows up for the delivery of your shipping containers, you will require to have a proper idea of the logistics of delivering the containers to a designated location. Once your delivery driver knows in detail about the location and how they can reach there, they will be able to develop a plan of how to deliver the shipping containers to your designated location. Having some idea about the location in advance will allow the delivery person to consider additional tools and equipment that they might require for making the job easier. The desired spots of your windows and doors on the shipping containers are also required to be discussed with the delivery person. It is especially the case when you tend to do everything on your own.

It is a crucial step as the way the containers are loaded on the truck will impact how it comes off at the time of delivery. Once your shipping containers reach the site, there will be no easy of turning and rotating the containers if you do not want to get a contractor. So, ensure that you discuss every possible detail with the delivery person before they even arrive at your desired location.

Choosing The Method Of Delivery

One of the most common ways of delivering shipping containers to any location is by the help of trucks. However, there are certain options relying on the style or size of the shipping containers. Two of the standard trailer options are:

- Tile-bed trailer

- Flatbed trailer

Now, which one is a better option for delivering your trucks? Everything will depend on the equipment you have at the delivery site along with your budget. For instance, a tilt-bed trailer might turn out to be a great option when you do not have a forklift or crane designated for the shape and size of your shipping containers. A tilt-bed trailer will allow the delivery person to drop off the containers in the designated spot without the need for any extra equipment. There is a consideration that you need to be aware of while opting for tilt-bed trailers – they can only accommodate containers between 20 feet and 40 feet.

The second option is a flatbed trailer. It is the least expensive option; however, it will need extra equipment and tools, along with a crane or forklift. All the additional equipment will incur more charges. Once you are determined about the location where you want to place the shipping containers, you can be sure if the cost-saving while using the flatbed option is a better option in comparison to the tilt-bed one.

Land Preparation For Your Shipping Containers

Before the delivery truck gets your shipping containers to the location, the land where they are meant to be placed needs to be ready for the placement of the containers. Once shipping containers are delivered, there is no possible easy way of moving them so that you can make adjustments. The ground of placing the shipping containers needs to be completely firm and flat. If you fail to provide your containers a proper base, you might run the risk of structurally compromising the overall integrity of your home. Also, having an uneven surface might hugely impact the containers even before they are properly placed on the ground.

Another essential element that you need to consider is the risk of potential flooding. Even when you do not have any plans of placing the shipping containers near any water surface, you need to allow proper drainage of water much away from the containers. It indicates that if you tend to place the containers in low-lying areas, even a slight elevation near the containers might result in a huge disaster if there is snow or rain. In fact, improper drainage might impact the quality of your home foundation. If you fail to have a designated way for water to leave the home area, you will risk softening up the foundation that is placed under the containers. It might be the case the shipping containers start sinking into the ground. It will create an unsafe structure for your home. Depending on the conditions of the ground, you can opt for several normal foundation options.

- Hard grass
- Gravel
- Cement
- Compact dirt

- Pavement

If you are not willing to use any of these traditional foundations, you can opt for the advanced foundation options that we discussed in the earlier chapters. They need to be placed under the shipping container corners. The aim is to lift up the containers from the ground and avoid sinking.

If you do not mind paying a bit extra, a chassis will be a great option for you. It will allow you to move the shipping containers at any time in the future. It is a kind of foundation used for securing a shipping container in place at the time of transportation.

What Do You Need To Do On The Day Of Delivery?

The day of delivery has arrived, and it is obviously an exciting step in the entire process of building your shipping container home. You will have to pay attention to certain logistical considerations in relation to delivery. The most important thing to keep in mind is that the delivery trailer and truck will be large in size. Make sure they can reach up to the location of delivery and also get out properly.

CHAPTER 10

ROOFING STYLES FOR YOUR HOME

The choice of whether you should add a roof to your shipping container home or not is made up of two things – the cost and personal preference. It is quite clear that not opting for container roofing will surely save you some money in the initial stages. But in the long run, getting a roof and insulating it properly can help you a lot save money on your energy bills. As hot air rises, most of the heat that is lost in your home will be because of it escaping through the roof. At the time of making this decision, you will have to consider the fact that getting a roof will allow you to insulate the inner portion of the roof. It will help in maintaining and keeping the internal temperature of the home consistent. Also, having a shipping container roof with an overhang will help in keeping the rain running down onto the windows. It will also discard the need to get a drip bar above all the windows.

Styles Of Roofing

When it comes to roofing your shipping container home, there are various choices for you. The one that you choose needs to be determined properly before you install the same.

Shed

In a shed-style roof, a sloped roof is used. One of the primary advantages of getting a shed-style roof is that it is quite cheap and is also easy to build. Such a roof can be designed, built, and installed within a few days. In fact, if you want to use solar energy for your home, the sloping, long roof will allow you to install solar panels with ease. In order to install a shed-style roof on your container home, you will have to start by welding right-angled steel plates all across the length of the container on both sides. On both sides of the container roof, attach one wooden beam to the plates. Now, screw the trusses into the beam. The basic structure of the roof is already taking shape. You can add steel bars or purlins across the trusses for structural support.

The roof structure will be more or less complete. You can add purlins of 20 feet across the trusses for this stage, and you are good to go. Now, you will have to get braces for the trusses so that you protect them from strong wind. It is when you will need a structural engineer for the specifics. A professional engineer can provide you with all the necessary advice regarding the load-bearing capacity that is required for the roof. It will vary, especially regionally, as it depends on natural stresses that are imposed on the roof, like wind, snow, and rain loads. For covering the roof, you can use shingles, coated steel sheets, or galvanized metal sheets. Generally, coated steel sheets will be more durable. But if you opt for galvanized metal sheets, you can fit them quite easily and are pretty durable as well.

The final stage is to ensure that the roof has enough ventilation. In order to do this, the roof trusses need to overhang outside the container boundary. You can attach a soffit and fascia board under the trusses. A soffit board will need to have a minimum of a one-inch gap right in the middle, covered using wire mesh, that will permit air to flow in and out of the container roof. You will have to ensure that you permit ventilation at the gable ends. You can do this by cutting slots using a disc cutter out of steel. It will permit air to pass through and also prevent condensation and heat traps that lead to rusting.

Gable

The next option that you have got is to opt for a gable-style roof. It is the most common type of roof that the majority of people can think of while talking about traditional home roofing. It comes with a distinguishing triangle look. One of the advantages of installing a gable roof is that it includes sloped roofs on both sides that allow proper drainage of water. It will make sure that water does not leak and also helps in extending the overall lifespan of the roof. It is quite popular as it will provide you with lots of ceiling space compared to other roofing styles. The construction process of this kind of roof is more or less similar to that of the shed roof. For the installation of a gable roof on your container home, you will have to weld steel plates at right angles across the shipping container length on both sides.

On the sides of the roof, attach one wooden beam to the plates. Screw the trusses into the wooden beams, and the basic structure is ready. Next, attach purlins for completing the structure of the roof. Just like a shed roof, you can use any of these: coated steel sheets galvanized metal sheets, or shingles. You will need to ensure that there is enough ventilation. Again, trusses need to overhang the boundary of the container. Now, you can install a soffit board under the trusses. You will have to maintain a one-inch gap in the middle of the soffit board.

Flat

A flat roof is the one that a shipping container already comes with. It can be sufficient for the needs of some people. It can also be opted for when you are running on a tight budget. Indeed, it is very cheap in comparison to the other options; however, it might leave you with water pooling right on the flat surface of the roof. In case you make up your mind not to add roofing to your shipping container home, you will have to install a quick safety barrier. You can lay a sheet of tarpaulin on the surface of the roof and then overlay the same with asphalt rolls. It will help in adding a layer of defense between the roof of your house and dampness.

Importance Of Consulting A Structural Engineer

No matter which kind of roof you opt for, ensure that you work with a structural engineer. They can help you to calculate the load-bearing capacity and requirements for the roof. In order to do this, a structural engineer will calculate the live, dead, and transient load of the roof.

- The live load will include the weight of any tools and people who work to install the roof.

- The dead load will include the combined weight of all kinds of materials used to build the roof, like purlins, roof tiles, and trusses.

- The transient load will include all the natural stresses that are placed on the roof, like wind, snow, and rain.

The load-bearing capacity is the overall capacity of the roof that it can hold without collapsing. Each regional area will tend to face different challenges. For example, areas that are prone to strong winds will require roofs with extra bracing for the installed trusses. No matter which kind of roof you opt for, you will have to ensure adequate ventilation.

CHAPTER 11

FLOORING FOR YOUR HOME

Moving to the stage of flooring is an exciting stage. You will start seeing your new home taking proper shape by this point. Just like with every other step of the process, you have got a number of options. In simple terms, no matter which way you decide to go about it, you will have to deal with two steps: dealing with the actual flooring and preparing the finished flooring. When you get your shipping container, it will come with a plywood floor already installed. You might get tempted to keep the existing flooring; however, there are certain things that you will have to keep in mind. The preinstalled floors are treated with various hazardous chemicals along with pesticides. All such chemicals might get into your house interior and lead to health hazards.

So, the existing floor will have to be removed and replaced. Or, you can seal the same before moving ahead. If you are getting brand new containers for your home, you have got one more option. You can ask the company to deliver the containers without any kind of flooring. It will save you a lot of time in this stage; however, new containers are always more expensive. The last option that you can opt for is getting prefab containers where everything will be taken care of.

Removal Of Existing Flooring

One of the primary things that you will have to remember is that while sourcing your shipping containers, you will have to check the condition of the flooring. If it is possible for you to examine by yourself, you will have to check for dents, holes, cracks, or any other type of damage. If you can check it yourself, you are left with no other option other than relying on the inspection of the supplier. If the existing flooring is damaged, there is no other option aside from the removal of the floor. Keep in mind that if you opt for this path, you will also have to consider the cost of the plywood in your budget. Getting rid of the existing floor is not that tough. But it will take some sweat and time. After you are done with the process of removal, you will have to fix your new flooring. Always handle the task of flooring first before going for the interior.

Getting A Subfloor

If the existing flooring is not damaged, and if there is no need to remove the same, you can get a subfloor. The main purpose of this stage is to ensure that the harmful chemicals in the already existing floor are not getting into your space of living. So, the first step in laying a subfloor is to properly seal the existing floor. For sealing, you will have to clean the floor using isopropyl alcohol. After this, coat the floor with low-viscosity epoxy. It works great in damp places and also when the level of moisture is quite high. The next step after sealing is to place a layer of plywood. Getting three-quarter-inch plywood can do the job perfectly. You can also opt for tongue and groove sheets. After you are done with placing the sheets, drill through the sheets into the original flooring. If you want, you can also install a half-inch layer of foam over the sealed flooring before getting the new plywood flooring. It will help in adding more insulation.

The only issue with getting a subfloor is that it will raise the height. You will lose about one inch from the original height of your interior space.

Concrete Flooring

It is the last option of dealing with the existing flooring. If you opt for this, you are not required to seal the existing floor. You will also not need to get a subfloor. You can add concrete to the existing floor directly. It will automatically act as a sealing layer. Concrete is a great option for flooring in a variety of ways. It is easy to clean, lasts long enough, and can be designed in plenty of ways. You can also dye the floor by adding some color, polishing the floor to get a sparkling finish, or opting for textures or patterns. Well, there are certain disadvantages too. Concrete might absorb a lot of cold during lower temperatures. So, it might get chilly on the feet. It will also be increasing your heating costs. You will also have to get steel reinforcement in place for providing flexural strength.

One of the best ways of setting up steel for the flooring is by welding steel bars of 2 mm across the width and length of the flooring. You will have to set them one inch above existing flooring. After you are done with welding, you are all set to pour.

Finishing Flooring

For all the options that have been mentioned above, you will have to ensure that they are done before dressing and framing the interior. If you want to opt for concrete flooring, it can be used as finished flooring. But the other options will need a proper finish that will look good and also fits with the interior. There are various options for finishing your flooring. You can opt for carpet, tile, or laminate. One of the primary things that you will have to consider while choosing your flooring is the temperature of the location. If your location is hot, for instance, you will need something that will help cool down your home. Tile and laminate are good choices for this. They will help in maintaining a cool temperature besides keeping the floor surface comfortable while the outside temperature is quite high.

If your home location is quite cold, opting for carpeting can benefit you. Although it is a more challenging option to clean, it feels a lot better on your feet when the outside temperature is freezing. You will be able to hold the warmth inside your home, thus cutting down the heating costs. No matter which option you choose, you will have to start by properly measuring the floor. It will help you to know what you will need to purchase in terms of materials. You will have to get the overall square footage of your floor space. In case you are opting for carpet, you will need to prepare your space using carpet grippers. They are thin wooden strips that come with sharp pins on one side. The purpose of carpet grippers is to hold the edges of the carpet in their place. Line the room edges with carpet grippers and once you are happy with the placement, nail the carpet into the flooring with the grippers.

Opting for tile is also a great option. It is hassle-free when it comes to cleaning, and it can also be set in pretty patterns. It is a perfect fit for warmer climates. Tiling is an art in itself. You can start by laying the tiles row by row as you will be working on a rectangular container. If you want to opt for laminate flooring, you will need to work on it after you are done framing the home interior. You can place laminates over a subfloor or over concrete flooring. The majority of the laminate flooring comes in groove and tongue boards. So, it is an easy thing to fit each board into the other. While working with laminate, you will have to fit the edges to space. In simple terms, if you tend to opt for installing laminate before framing the walls, you might have to cut the laminate around the wall corrugations.

You can play around with the flooring style of your container home and work on the same for matching the interior designs. But no matter which option you choose, sealing the existing floor is of prime importance if you are not removing it.

CHAPTER 12

MAKING YOUR HOME INTERIOR AND EXTERIOR UNIQUE

Style is the appearance aesthetic of a shipping container house, as it is positioned and designed. The two elements, in conjunction, lead to a great-looking shipping container house that cannot be compared to the alternatives. While talking of design, there are two viewpoints – the exterior and interior of the building. In real life, there are various ways of affecting each of which you might not have stressed upon.

Home Interior

In general, the interior of a shipping container home that is unmodified includes white walls along with a roof. It might look bare and industrial; however, it can be made quite modern with the perfect style. There are homeowners who like to maintain the original floors and walls. But introducing new materials is also common. An alternative option to original walls is sheet metal or gypsum board that helps in creating flat and uniform walls. You can paint them and also texture the same in combination with bedding and taping. You can also opt for other wall options, like beach board, plywood, wooden planks, and cement panels. If you find the original flooring of the container unsatisfactory, you have got the option of flooring. You can use any kind of material like brick, concrete, tapestry, wood, vinyl, and others.

There are a number of choices for your roof as well. You can use the same material just like your wall or use something else to give the interior a contrasting look. But if you want to have bigger rooms, you will have to raise the ceiling and break off the walls between connecting bins.

Home Exterior

Getting exterior insulation is always a good idea. Well, you have got some other options too for finishing the exterior walls of your container home if you use spray foam. You can easily paint over the layer of insulation or even add a stucco for covering the same. What is important is to keep the insulation covered and sealed so that you can save it from external conditions and direct sunlight. Painting is a superb approach for finishing the external walls of your container home. However, you will need to be specific about the nature of the paints that you use. If you paint over spray foam insulation, you will either have to use latex paint or water-based acrylic paint. Stay away from oil-based paint as it might damage the insulation.

Stuccoing the external walls of your container home looks good and is a great option for you to consider. But if you want to use stucco on spray foam, make sure that the insulation layer has rough edges so the stucco can attach more easily.

Appealing Layouts

Shipping container homes are quite flexible in nature, and you can use them to make almost everything you can think of. One of the unique features of shipping containers is that they are stable and weatherproof in nature. All you need to do is to tweak them a bit and make everything look fine. You can stack and combine shipping containers to create a better-designed home. With shipping containers, you can cut the inner walls and also open them up to create enormous spaces for living. It is an easy task to lay doors, major openings, or an arch for connecting several containers in a horizontal manner. You can also combine containers vertically. You can stack ten or more containers, and that will depend on the way they are filled.

Family Compound

The layout that we will cover here is known as the family compound. But it does not have anything to be used by families only. The idea of this layout takes full advantage of the fact that shipping containers can be treated as complete units. In place of trying to combine the containers for making larger buildings, you will be forming a compound with various separate containers. You can place the containers as close enough as you feel like. But try not to place them more than a hundred feet apart. Such a layout will provide you lots of privacy along with separation. You will also be close enough for going back and forth the entire day. The shipping containers are separated by their functions. Each member of the family will have their own container room along with a bathroom. You can share the kitchen and living room in one single container.

Another alternative is to put two bedrooms in each container, a bathroom and kitchen in one container, and dining and living areas in another container. In case you need a larger living area, you can combine multiple containers while using the single containers for the smaller rooms. It all depends on the way you want to design your compound. In the majority of cases, covered walkways are provided between the containers so that you can easily move around, regardless of the external conditions. Opting for a family compound will make it easy for you to add to the overall size of your 'house' compound as the situation changes with time, such as elderly parents, children, or businesses based on home. You will also have the flexibility of shutting down parts of your compound when they are not in use or based on the seasons.

Most of the shipping container homeowners tend to spend a majority of their time in the outside transition spaces for reading, meals, relaxing, and other activities. The common outside area can be used like a porch, where you can have access to fresh smells of nature, fresh air, and nature sounds while staying protected from the intense heat of the sun. Well, a family compound might not be a great idea for all kinds of habitats. However, there is a considerable time of the year in the majority of the world where the outside temperatures are quite tolerable, if not enjoyable.

Shipping container homes will provide you with the freedom of creating almost any kind of house that you want. If budget is not an issue, you can also experiment with the designs to find out the perfect one.

CHAPTER 13

BUILDING REGULATIONS

Shipping containers, no matter if you use them for your living space or only as a shipping unit, are subject to several types of city codes and laws. You will also have to understand that it is not only a matter of getting certain approvals from the local authorities. A shipping container home building permit or code ensures that you have a building inspector who is accredited by the city authority for verifying the integrity of all your building plans. An inspector will examine the location of the container, position, and several other things. The checks are meant to tackle a number of topics.

- The rigidity of the surface – to make sure that the soil is enough for supporting the weight of the container/containers

- Structure security

- Snow accumulation

- Uplift or overturning risk

- Wind resistance

- Enough anchorage

Here are certain things that might affect the permits in the state.

- The actual location of the container on the premises

- Local laws and ordinances

- The physical state of the container/containers

- The planned time period of construction

- The effect of the container on the attitudes of the neighbors or community

So, what are the possible shipping container home permit conditions that a homeowner needs to be aware of?

Shipping Container Home Building Regulations

Shipping containers, just like any other conventional house, need to be designed in proper compliance with strict permits and legislation. In order to make sure proper licensing, you will have to ensure that the building structure is appropriately zoned. Once you are done with zoning, you will have to keep the following in mind, depending on the city zoning laws.

Property zoning

Zoning indicates the segmentation of property in various parts in order to properly specify the types of buildings that can be developed or built. Generally, a process controlled by the government, zoning of land helps in planning the development of metropolitan regions. It is a method the government for grouping all kinds of density-controlled related systems. Property zoning is essential for any kind of building project. So, ensure that the correct zoning laws of your area influence the location of the shipping container/containers.

Building permits and codes

The next important shipping container regulation is building permits and codes. Also, it is one of the most important steps before you can install your shipping container. You will require a building license for showing compliance with the building codes that are applicable. By adopting construction approvals and codes of the government, all kinds of architectural requirements are upheld. The International Residential Code (IRC) and the International Building Code (IBC) are based on the licenses and building codes. All these uniform regulatory bodies come with strict rules on fire safety, power, and plumbing inside residential buildings. Such codes are often revised after every few years. Shipping container homes might also be subject to various licenses and standards that will depend on the municipal authorities. So, ensure that you get in touch with the local authorities with the updated policy.

There are some US states that have their very own codes, like the Massachusetts State Building Code. However, what applies to someone might not just matter to you. You are required to be concerned with the regulations that are specific to your area. Understanding and finding all these rules right before you can start with your construction is an essential step. In case you have some doubt, you can get in touch with a professional like a general contractor or an architect in your locality. The last thing that anyone would like to do is to ignore the pertaining rules. Depending on the case, you might end up with additional fees, penalties, stopped construction, or even orders for tearing down and starting over.

Common Shipping Container Home Items That Get Regulated

There are several variabilities regarding who regulates what in relation to shipping container buildings. So, instead of describing the regulatory practices of so many entities, let us have a look at the list of various types of things that might get regulated when it comes to shipping container homes. Completely depending on the place where you live, all, some, or even none of these might apply to you. The rules might be from any kind of combination of building codes, property zoning, and others.

- **Appearance:** Style, color, roof, wall materials, and any other kind of external parts of the house

- **Size:** Number of bedrooms, square footage, maximum allowed height, and others

- **Accessibility:** Requirements linked to making the home accessible to all those with disabilities

- **Foundation:** Depth, type, height over the ground to prevent flooding, and others

- **Site offsets:** Distance from the neighboring structures, distance from the line of property to the house edge, and others

- **Landscaping:** Plant types that are permitted, the total number of trees that can be removed at the time of construction, and others

- **Smoke and fire protection:** Type, number, and location of carbon monoxide detectors, smoke detectors, and others

- **Structure:** Requirements for dealing with snow and wind loads, necessary structural reinforcements, and others

- **Energy conservation:** Particular requirements in regards to certain things like insulation, windows, appliances, sealing around penetrations, and others for reducing energy usage

Again, the applicability of all these will depend on your location.

Regulating Bodies

Each region of your country will be different from the other in regards to which level of the government has jurisdiction. There are several levels of government that you will have to work with – county, municipal, federal, and state. Generally, the regulations from the higher-order entities will apply along with the lowest level having jurisdiction. For instance, in a city, all four kinds of regulations will apply.

Municipal regulation

While talking about municipal government, we only mean towns and cities. They develop rules that tend to pertain to the land area that is within their bounds. Cities keep annexing new land into the city from time to time. If your location is quite old and outside the city limits, there is no need to comply with the regulations. But it is always better to ask about future annexation while purchasing new land. Most of the building codes in the US are enforced at the level of municipal government.

County regulation

It is the next step right after municipalities. While there are not many properties within a city, every property that can be found in the US is a county. Completely depending on how urban the county is, it will be more or less regulated in regards to the regulations of building a home. In some other countries, there exist similar regulations like a county, but that might subdivide into sub-regions.

State regulation

In the US, the majority of state governments do not have much to do in regards to building regulations. However, there are certain notable exceptions for certain things, such as earthquake requirements in California, hurricane requirements in Florida, and others.

Federal regulation

The US Federal Government does not have much to do with building regulations. In other countries, it is possible that the majority of the regulations are made at the national or federal level.

It will be better for you if you can familiarize yourself first with the municipal guidelines of your area before you can expand your knowledge about the county, state, and federal regulations.

CHAPTER 14

COMMONLY MADE MISTAKES

It is often said that shipping containers can be a suitable building block for developing new homes or offices. Although it is true, there are certain shortcomings and pitfalls of any kind of building construction material or method. People tend to jump into shipping container home projects without even opting for proper research first. As a result, they tend to run into various types of issues that could be avoided if you can get the necessary knowledge beforehand. We will discuss some of the common shipping container home mistakes in this chapter and how to deal with the same.

Failing To Understand The Building Regulations And Rules

It does really matter where you are planning to construct your shipping container home; there will be regulations that you need to follow. Well, the rules and regulations tend to differ from country to country and community to community. Try not to depend on any kind of second-hand information. You will have to do your own research and get in touch with state and local authorities to ensure that your new home is compliant when you are at the stage of planning. Never try to do this when you are already halfway through. You might need to tear down everything and restart again. It will be easier and cost-effective to opt for new changes in your plans while discussing with your contractor and engineer in comparison to doing the same once it is in place and fixed. You will have to take out some time to get done with this crucial step so that you can prevent all kinds of future hassles.

Opting For The Wrong Container Type

Not being able to choose the right shipping container might turn out to be a big mistake. You will have to ensure that you have some proper plans in your mind and follow the same while looking out for your containers. Try not to compromise on the size of the containers, as you can select containers ranging from 20 feet to 40 feet. You might also want to opt for open-top variants at the time of getting your containers. Additionally, it will be better for you if you try not to settle for the regular height. High cube containers are about one foot higher in comparison to the regular ones. They will provide you with more headroom along with more space for insulation.

Neglecting Insulation

If you fail to insulate your container home properly, you might have to face some extreme conditions, depending on your area's climate. Shipping containers are generally designed for the transportation of goods and not for maintaining a constant temperature. It indicates that unless you insulate your shipping container home properly, it will be super hot during the summer and cold in the winter. Generally, homeowners opt for spray foam insulation. If your home location receives a lot of rain, having the proper insulation will help in creating a proper barrier against vapor. If your area is dry and warm, stay away from vapor barriers. There are other insulation options as well that you can try out.

Getting Used Containers Without Inspection

Shipping containers go through a lot when in usage, like being lashed out by sea waves or getting knocked down by transporters. You can never find two used shipping containers being the same. You will have to take some time to understand the various grading conditions while getting second-hand containers. Try to inspect the containers by yourself before getting them. Also, opt for reputable companies for getting your containers. You are also required to research the provider of the containers. Building a container home indicates that you would like to save. So, it will be better for you if you can search for companies that will offer you wholesale rates.

Cutting Out A Lot Of Steel

One of the primary advantages of shipping container homes is its strength. It does not matter how creative you want to be with your shipping container home. Cutting out lots of steel from the containers will be compromising the overall structural strength. Indeed, they are modular units that can be easily stacked over each other. However, over-modification might turn out to be dangerous. Try working on the interiors instead. Cutting out steel for installing windows and doors is surely safe. But in case you need to cut out more than that, you will have to opt for reinforcement. You can get extra support from steel beams, but they will cost you extra.

Planning House On Poor Foundation

Right before anything else, the foundation of your home comes first for any kind of construction. You might not be much aware, but the foundation is one of the key components while building your shipping container home. When the foundation is improper, you might easily run into problems related to container homes. The nature of the ground is something that you will have to consider before you can start building. Sinking and sliding might take place any time, which might even result in the separation of your shipping container home. The composition of the ground will affect the way in which your container home reacts. So, before you start building, stress on the foundation of your container home. When you have a well-constructed foundation, it will ensure equal weight distribution throughout the space of your home.

CHAPTER 15

FREQUENTLY ASKED QUESTIONS

Just like any other topic in the world, there are certain questions that are commonly asked all the time. We will discuss some of the frequently asked questions in this chapter so that your journey of building a shipping container home gets easier.

Is There A Chance Of Getting Baked Inside A Shipping Container Home In Hot Weathers?

Well, the answer is no. Generally, any kind of structural base, be it concrete, wood, steel panels, or blocks, have the chance of getting hot in higher temperatures. Every structure needs proper ventilation and insulation. As long as you can maintain proper insulation and ventilation of your shipping container home, you will not have any kind of problems related to temperature regulation.

In Which States Can I Build Shipping Container Homes?

Some of the states that are the most receptive for shipping container homes are:

- California
- Missouri
- Louisiana
- Alaska
- Texas
- Tennessee
- Oregon

The majority of the states will allow you to build shipping container homes; however, the governing authorities will determine the requirements and regulations. Make sure you schedule lots of project time as the approval process for container homes might be longer than traditional homes.

Will My Shipping Container Home Rust And Corrode?

Remember that shipping containers are built for the transportation of goods across the ocean. It indicates that they are designed for saltwater and humidity. Shipping containers are built from special kinds of steel that are non-corrosive. They also come with a ceramic coating that makes them rustproof virtually. So, it can be said that your shipping container home will not rust and corrode with proper care.

Is It Possible To Get Financing For My Shipping Container Home?

Getting financing for your shipping container home might turn out to be a challenging task. The majority of the lending institutions are not that compliant to take the risk of alternative homes. You can seek the advice of some established shipping container home builders to get knowledge about viable options. You might also consult a personal loan expert.

How Long Will A Shipping Container Home Last?

The average lifespan of shipping container homes is around 30 and 50 years. You can increase the lifespan if the containers are well-treated, properly insulated, properly maintained, includes external wall cladding, and are located in a proper climate. A proper estimate for a shipping container home would be to minus the service years of your bought containers from 25 years. One of the major concerns of shipping container homes is the short life expectancy. Continuous maintenance to prevent corrosion and rust will have to be included in your building plans and designs. You will have to address all kinds of issues with proper care for increasing the lifespan of your container home.

Will My Shipping Container Home Hold Any Value?

There is no form of any historical data of the market that can help in estimating the appreciation or depreciation of any shipping container home. In order to properly hedge the risk of depreciating asset, you will have to place the containers at a place that have chances of appreciating with time. Container homes generally involve some degree of risk because of: shorter lifespan, chances of rust, feature and size limitations, and also competitive alternatives. As a shipping container home ages, it might tend to be less desirable for prospective buyers. You can get in touch with a local agent, specifically if shipping container homes are prevalent in the area.

Is Any Permit Required For Building A Shipping Container Home?

While building a container home, you will require permits for all those things that you generally need for any kind of traditional buildings. But before you get your land, try to check with the county or city authorities to determine if there is any restriction or requirement to develop a shipping container home. Make sure that you opt for experienced shipping container home contractors or engineers to adhere to the best practices. Before your shipping containers reach the building site, you need to get done with these tasks – land purchase, building permits, and construction of the foundation. Restrictive zoning and planning boards might need a site survey, structural engineering reports, and architectural design review before you can start with any kind of actual construction. In case your county does not have much experience with shipping container homes, you can expect repeated visits and delays before getting a green signal.

Are Container Homes Sustainable?

Some of the reasons why shipping container homes cannot be regarded to be sustainable are:

- **Premature recycling:** Used containers often get recycled too soon as there are various homes that are built with only single-use containers.

- **Remnant toxins:** The majority of the shipping containers get treated with toxic paints along with toxic chemicals for the flooring to maintain durability. Also, there are containers that carried toxic cargo.

- **Inefficient recycling:** One shipping container, if only recycled as steel, can yield plenty of metal studs for building fourteen houses of the exact same size in comparison to container homes.

- **COR-TEN steel:** There are shipping containers made from COR-TEN steel, which has lots of environmental baggage, along with corrosion and rust.

As most of the shipping container homes that you can find are made with used containers, there are industry practitioners who see this as a type of upcycling. But this form of upcycling is quite inefficient, provided the reasons above.

Can Shipping Container Homes Turn Out To Be Toxic?

The sole purpose of shipping containers is to transport goods for as many trips as they can. In order to improve their durability, containers are often treated with toxic chemicals. They are not really manufactured for being used as living spaces. Also, the containers might get used for the transportation of toxic goods. The paint used on the walls is very tough and contains loads of chemical compounds that someone would not want in their house. It is always suggested to sand down the existing paints, down to the layer of the raw steel.

You can also add extra layers on the walls and floors for sealing the toxic materials.

Do I Need To Get A Foundation For My Shipping Container Home?

Yes, you will need a proper foundation for your container home for two reasons.

- You cannot allow steel to touch the ground as the moisture from the ground might lead to rusting.

- The shipping container needs to be placed on a stable and non-shifting base.

Is Shipping Container Home A Bad Choice?

Generally, shipping container homes are suggested when you have a tight budget. But they are often considered to be bad investments for having:

- Minimal cost saving

- Short lifespan

- Fewer options of financing

- Small spaces for living

- Reduced integrity of the structure

- Long approval and permitting processes

- Limited option for future changes or modifications

Whether you want to get a shipping container home or not can be easily determined by going through all the above-mentioned answers.

CONCLUSION

Thank you for making it through to the end of the *Shipping Container Homes*; let's hope it was informative and able to provide you with all of the tools you need to achieve your goals, whatever they may be.

I hope that you found this guidebook to be exactly what you were searching for. As you are now acquainted with all sorts of necessary information related to shipping container homes, you can easily build one. Not only can you use shipping containers for building a home, but you can also them for any other kind of building purpose. If you are tight on your budget, getting a shipping container home might turn out to be a great idea. Besides everything, this guidebook also provided you with lots of ideas related to flooring, insulation, and also every possible thing that you need to keep in mind while designing your home.

Keep in mind that proper and thorough research can turn out to be your best friend when you are opting for a new type of house. Try to consider the location, weather, and condition of the place that you choose for building your container home. Do not forget to get some proper ideas about the regulations of your area. The key here is to have everything in place so that you can easily avoid any kind of future alterations or issues. Shipping container homes are easily customizable. So, you can unleash your creative side while designing your new home.

Finally, if you found this book useful in any way, a review on Amazon is always appreciated!

Made in the USA
Monee, IL
19 October 2021

44cb9312-efdd-4f14-a2ad-5489732631e9R01